MW01040352

# CARTOON MAGIC

## HOW TO HELP CHILDREN DISCOVER THEIR RAINBOWS WITHIN

# CARTOON MAGIC

## HOW TO HELP CHILDREN DISCOVER THEIR RAINBOWS WITHIN

Richard J. Crowley, Ph.D.
Joyce C. Mills, Ph.D.

Magination Press
A DIVISION OF BRUNNER/MAZEL, INC.
New York

**Library of Congress Cataloging-in-Publication Data**

Crowley, Richard J., 1942–
    Cartoon magic.

    1. Children's drawings—Psychological aspects.
2. Cartoon characters—Psychological aspects.
3. Cartoons and children.   4. Imagination in
children.   5. Child psychology.   6. Child rearing.
I. Mills, Joyce., 1944–    . II. Title.
BF723.D7C76   1988      618.92'891656      88-8386
ISBN 0-945354-07-X

Copyright © 1989 by Richard J. Crowley and Joyce C. Mills

*Published by*
**Magination Press**
An Imprint of Brunner/Mazel, Inc.,
19 Union Square West, New York, NY 10003

*Distributed in Canada by*
**Book Center**
1140 Beaulac St., Montreal, Quebec H4R 1R8, Canada

MANUFACTURED IN THE UNITED STATES OF AMERICA

10   9   8   7   6   5   4   3   2

*To all the rainbows*
*that touch the earth*
*in so many ways.*

# CONTENTS

# FOREWORD

*Cartoon Magic* by Richard J. Crowley and Joyce C. Mills at last gives parents a wealth of easy, creative techniques that *they* can use to help their children. The focus of these techniques is the use of cartoon characters as "home remedies" that can guide children in finding solutions to a variety of difficulties, ranging from nightmares, to hospital visits, to the loss of a friend or pet.

Their delightful presentation leads parents back to the land of their own imaginations and helps them reenter the world of the child. Once in this world where "pretend" rules, parents can use the specific, step-by-step instructions that accompany the "Pretend Techniques" to direct their children toward positive problem solving.

Many case examples give readers a sense of the very real ways in which these techniques can be applied, and reproductions of children's actual drawings provide added power and poignancy.

A helpful "Cartoon Rating Scale" completes this valuable book and gives parents an easy way to identify the most positive cartoon characters for their children.

Crowley and Mills view parents as "powerful, positive agents of change." *Cartoon Magic* makes it possible for parents who aren't feeling particularly powerful and positive to be what the authors say they are. Everyone loves fantasizing, and this book should help us raise our children in a manner compatible with our fantasy.

*Arnold Zukow, M.D.*
*Chief of Pediatrics*
*Tarzana Hospital*
*Tarzana, California*

A gentle spring shower blends with the warm rays of the sun; ribbons of colors streaming across the sky create a natural beauty to behold...a beauty known as a rainbow.

# CARTOON MAGIC

## HOW TO HELP CHILDREN DISCOVER THEIR RAINBOWS WITHIN

# 1
# CARTOON FRIENDS

# "Scooby Doo to the Rescue"

Five-year-old Davey was having violently fearful nightmares. His parents reported how he would awaken each night screaming uncontrollably, "The monsters are getting me!" They had tried everything they could think of, but nothing worked. They now felt frustrated and helpless in their inability to comfort their little boy.

While the parents were present in the session, we asked Davey if he could draw a picture of the monster. He eagerly picked up the markers and began his drawing. (Figure 1) We then asked him to draw a picture of his favorite cartoon friend, one that he knew could help him with the monster. His eyes widened as he exclaimed, "It's Scooby Doo!" His parents were puzzled by this; they thought that Scooby scared Davey because of the ghosts in the stories. At that point Davey blurted out, "Oh no! Scooby makes the ghosts go away!" We commented to the parents that as adults sometimes we need to remember how to see things through a child's eyes. Davey picked up an orange marker and painstakingly began to draw Scooby Doo. (Figure 2)

**Figure 1**
Davey's Monster

**Figure 2**
Davey's Cartoon Helper, Scooby Doo

On a third sheet of paper, Davey was asked to draw how his problem would look "all better." He closed his eyes for a moment, then opened them wide and with enthusiasm drew his third picture. (Figure 3)

Davey's parents were instructed to put paper and markers in his room. When he awoke at night, crying and afraid, they were to help him employ the same drawing process. The parents were delighted to become a part of their son's healing process. They had anticipated many sessions of individual psychotherapy to "figure out" the problem. Instead, a total of nine sessions took place, during which straightforward information about the stages of child development was provided. During the final session, Davey drew how his nightmares used to look (Figure 4) and how his dreams looked in the present. (Figure 5)

In a follow-up call one month after therapy had been terminated, the parents reported no recurrence of the problem. Some six months later during a chance social encounter at a play one evening, Davey's parents again reported how well he was doing in school and that his sleep problems were "a thing of the past."

As parents, you may have all experienced that "What do we do now?" feeling when your child is struggling with a problem. In trying to find a special remedy to help your child, you might consult your

**Figure 3**
Davey's Problem "All Better"

**Figure 4**
Davey's Nightmare

8

**Figure 5**
Davey's Present Dream

collection of books on parenting by the many experts, you might call your pediatrician, or you might talk to a friend, relative or teacher. When your child is hurt by a minor cut or injury, the situation is easier. You first treat it with the basic home remedies you have available—antiseptics, bandaids and kisses. However, many of the problems encountered by children in our modern world are not so straightforward or easy to fix.

As two psychotherapists working in the often challenging and imaginative field of child psychology and hypnotherapy, we have found that cartoon characters can serve as invaluable "home remedies" to help your children solve a variety of everyday problems, difficulties and challenges.

At one time or another, all children have nightmares or fears of some kind. They experience the discomfort of minor childhood illnesses, some find themselves in hospitals undergoing major treatment, many fear a neighborhood bully, and all children face the challenge of schoolwork, classmates, and the ever-changing fabric of family life and relationships.

In traditional play therapy, children are given what is termed a "third medium" by which to work through the fears, tensions, aggressions and conflicts that naturally arise in their lives. This third medium may be drawing or playing with clay; it may be a sandbox full of dolls and toys; it may be the fairytales we all remember. Cartoon characters can also be added to this list, as an incredibly powerful third medium, which parents can use to help their children resolve their day-to-day problems of growing up in an ever-changing world. As parents help their children cope with and master the many challenges of childhood, the self-confidence that the children learn will give them that extra edge in entering the confusing world of adolescence and, eventually, adulthood.

Many of you reading this book no doubt remember hours of laughter and joy spent watching your favorite cartoon characters humorously get in and out of trouble each week on television or in the movies. You may even remember when you looked to that imaginary friend, whether it was Superman, Spider-Man, Wonder Woman, Mighty Mouse, or any other superhero, to give you the inner strength and resourcefulness you needed in a particular situation. Indeed, the Saturday morning cartoon shows and their entrancing array of cartoon friends provided a welcome staple in most of our childhoods.

Children truly see fun and humor in their cartoon friends. Numerous books use these cartoon friends to help children feel comfortable about going to the doctor or dentist. The themes are presented in humorous ways so that children begin to associate laughter with subjects that once frightened them. The humor and laughter can give the children another healthy coping skill for dealing with their hurts and illnesses.

There is increasing evidence from medical research that positive emotions and attitudes can have remarkable healing effects. That "laughter is the best medicine" was movingly demonstrated by Norman Cousins' experience of reversing an "irreversible" disease by watching old Marx Brothers films and Candid Camera reruns, along with sound medical treatment. In his search for self-healing, which he describes in his book *Anatomy of an Illness*, Cousins discovered that activating positive feelings could actually change the chemistry of his body. Similar results have been reported by the well-known researchers, the Simontons, in their book *Getting Well Again*. In their work with cancer patients, the Simontons have found that remission or containment of the cancer was directly related to how well the individual could visualize and believe in his or her own healing potentials. More recently, Bernie Siegel, in his book *Love, Medicine and Miracles*, movingly describes how what he terms "exceptional patients" can learn to take control and heal themselves from such life threatening illnesses as cancer by utilizing the power of positive attitudes, love, visualization and drawings in the healing process.

All parents want something better for their children. Because of this loving concern, you strive to the best of your abilities to create positive and enriching environments—the first toys carefully selected for your newborn, the many long hours spent guiding and nurturing your toddler, the school conferences, and all of the efforts to create optimal outer experiences for your children. While it is impossible to have complete control over all of the external experiences your children will encounter, it is possible for you to do a great deal toward fostering the inner resources and capabilities your children naturally possess and can use to cope with those outer experiences.

We believe that parents are powerful positive agents of change in their children's lives. With a number of simple "home remedies," parents can tap into their own creative sources, their own "inner guides," and find new ways of dealing with the problems their children encounter.

Children have the precious capacity of being able to enter spontaneously into worlds of their own making or worlds created for them. Whether fairy tales, movies or cartoons, children participate with a wonderment and openness lost to many of us as adults. As parents, you can create a special world utilizing the characters, story lines and settings of familiar cartoons and fantasy adventures which your children can enter for help and support when needed. These special worlds are like carefully designed fairytales, in which the "magical" can help solve the problems of everyday reality.

In our real world, we perceive a horse as just a horse. Yet, in the world of fantasy and mythology, with added wings, the horse becomes Pegasus, who can transport the beholder to all parts of the world in unlimited ways. How limited we really are by everyday reality. How incredibly free we become when entering the world of fantasy.

Our intention is to help each of you discover the wonderment of those fantasy cartoon characters who can serve as powerful "imaginary friends" for your children. Enjoy using the techniques in this book as your guide, and delight in seeing the beautiful colors of change emerge from within your child, just as colors emerge naturally through the soft mist of rain to form a rainbow, a rainbow that leads to the treasure within.

# 2
# LAND OF IMAGINATION

Since the first Mickey Mouse-Steamboat Willie cartoons, children throughout the world have enjoyed the fantasy creations provided by the art of animation. Little did Walt Disney realize that the playful cartoon characters he originally created solely for the purposes of entertainment and pleasure would become a fantastic vehicle for helping children with social, emotional, and medical problems. Today cartoon characters are used to teach children about environmental safety, drug and alcohol prevention, and how to deal with physical and emotional problems.

Parents can use this influence of cartoons creatively to help their children. How? By what power? By the power of childlike enthrallment. Even hyperactive children, unable to concentrate on their schoolwork for more than five minutes at a time, will baffle many by their ability to sit in rapt absorption for an hour or more of Saturday morning cartoons.

In entering the world of cartoons, children indeed enter an inner world all their own—a world of imagination and fantasy. In this special imaginary place, they become happily oblivious to the here-and-now world of everyday reality. The child's name can be called and there is no response; parents can even enter the room without rousing so much as a blink of recognition.

What a curious phenomenon this absorption is. Take a pleasant moment now to remember your own childhood worlds of storybooks, radio programs, television, and movies. Your might even recall this total absorption in current experiences from your adult life. How many times have you been so absorbed in a book that you were unaware of events around you? How many times have you found yourself daydreaming about a favorite place or vacation while working? Surely, both parents and children are able to remove themselves from an outer world of everyday reality to enter an inner world of imagination and fantasy. Not only is this world of imagination, pretending and daydreaming a natural ability experienced by all of us numerous times throughout the day, it is important for healthy child development. It can actually be the basis for much creative change.

The fantasy nature of cartoons and adventure stories can provide a focused stimulus for these experiences of inner absorption. In the movie *The Wizard of Oz*, Dorothy left her problems in the black and white world of Kansas to seek solutions in the colorful world of Oz. There Dorothy sought the help of her imaginary friends, Lion, Scarecrow, Tin Man, Glenda the good witch, and of course, the Wizard. It was through her experiences with each of these characters that Dorothy was able to discover the strengths she needed to confront her problems, which were symbolized by the wicked witch, and to learn that the answers always lay within her own self. In much the same way, children naturally leave their black and white world of everyday reality to enter a more colorful world of imagination. Here they are free to discover unexpected solutions which they can later apply to their problems in their here-and-now world.

Parents are often concerned about negative effects of cartoons or cartoon characters. Yet, *imaginatively applied* to the social and developmental problems common to all children, cartoons and cartoon characters can hold the key to positive change. It is our experience that every cartoon character can be utilized for positive effects. Yes, even the villains. For example, Joey, a child in the hospital who was battling pain, used the characters of his favorite cartoon show, Defenders of the Earth. He pretended that his pain was the villain, Ming the Merciless. Whenever the pain would begin to flare up, he would call upon the Defenders: Flash Gordon, The Phantom, Lothar, etc. This not only allowed him to disconnect from his pain as he entered his world of imagination, but more importantly gave him a sense of having control and playing an active role in his healing process.

Heroes or favorite cartoon characters can become children's imaginary friends throughout their hospital stay, accompanying them through each procedure. Of course, the strengths the children feel from their imaginary cartoon friends are their own inner strengths. Since children are not consciously aware of this ongoing parallel, they are free to imagine their cartoon friends having all the abilities and potentials that are really their own.

Those of us who have had the privilege of watching children play know that one true beauty of children is their ability to create joy out of something as ordinary as an old hat. They can play for hours, imagining it to be the pointed hat of a wonderful magic wizard or a crown for a king or queen. It is precisely this ability of children to create a world of imagination that can become a powerful healing element in both the common and the more serious problems of childhood.

By opening new doors of information and new approaches, we hope to stimulate parents to explore a new and exciting world of growth both for themselves and for their children. Using cartoons and their characters constructively involves learning to blend your own imaginative ideas with your children's ongoing creative abilities—abilities yet to be discovered.

# 3
# MATCHING

Matching is an important key to unlocking the beneficial effect cartoons and their characters can provide for your children, in much the same way that a spring shower precedes the ribbons of color that stream from the rainbow. In the early years of your children's education, much of the learning that takes place occurs through a matching process. The teacher presents an apple, a pear and a shoe, asking the children to match the two items that go together. Soon children learn that although an apple and pear are different, there is a relationship between them. They are both a type of fruit, whereas a shoe is a type of clothing. Children acquire this ability naturally during early developmental periods, and with each added year they become more adept at discriminating and matching.

In a similar way, children automatically identify with cartoon characters and stories that match their own situations. Even though the specific story ending presented in the cartoon may differ from the specifics of the children's lives, even though the cartoon character's personality may differ in obvious ways from the children's personalities, children have the natural ability to accept what relates to them (the apple and the pear) and reject what does not (the shoe).

In the Snoopy and Charlie Brown cartoons, for example, children know they are not Snoopy. Yet they may strongly identify with Snoopy's wonderful imaginative qualities, which help him solve any problem that comes his way. Snoopy's resourceful and light-hearted approach to life matches similar qualities of the children, and the children automatically make this connection. At the same time, Charlie Brown's endless insecurities also match children's pockets of fears, so another level of connection is made. Both strengths and weaknesses are thus represented in the lovable cartoon characters of Snoopy and Charlie Brown. (Figure 6)

This can be beneficial in two ways. While children are empathizing with Charlie Brown's latest catastrophe, they are also relating to Snoopy's cheerful attempts to teach Charlie Brown how to feel more confident and look on the bright side. At the same time that children's insecurities are validated in Charlie Brown's endearing flub-ups, their strengths are drawn out and activated by Snoopy's positive qualities.

There is yet another level to this example of

24

**Figure 6**
Snoopy and Charlie Brown, as drawn by 8-year-old Billy

matching. While Charlie Brown may portray children's more typical behavior, Snoopy portrays important potentials within the children they may not have learned to demonstrate, or may not even know they possess. Parents can learn to recognize when a cartoon character is matching their children's conscious abilities—the here-and-now world of typical, everyday behavior—and when the character is matching their unconscious potentials—those unique seeds of growth still hidden and unrecognized in their inner world of imagination. In this way, cartoons can actually help parents recognize in their children those subtle signals of emotional and social development most in need of support and nurturance.

The concept of matching can be demonstrated in the following example of an 11-year-old boy named Casey, who experienced difficulties in school. Whenever the teacher presented new math concepts to the class, Casey became worried and anxious about not being able to learn the new material. Casey was asked what cartoon character he would like to have with him when he became worried. Casey reported that he liked Rubik the Amazing Cube because Rubik knew how to help Carlos and the other kids in the cartoon when they were in trouble. Casey was asked to draw a picture of Rubik. After the drawing was completed, Casey was asked to imagine this new friend helping

**Figure 7**
Casey's Drawing of Rubik the Amazing Cube

27

him whenever he was worried about learning something new. Casey smiled and said he liked that idea. (Figure 7)

In this example, the cartoon characters who were having problems matched Casey's own problems; he identified with them. At the same time, Rubik the Amazing Cube also matched Casey's abilities and potentials, so without quite realizing it, Casey also strongly identified with Rubik.

Matching is what transforms an ordinary cartoon show into a source of help and growth. Only your children can determine which shows work for them. Two cartoon shows may appear to have similar characters and stories, yet children will respond to one but not the other. Trust that your children will select just the right shows and characters to match their own inner worlds.

# 4

# PRETENDING

Children use the World of Pretend and the World of Make-Believe intuitively. They know how to enter those worlds automatically. Nobody has to teach them. It appears to be a natural ability (and resource) that evolved on its own and is applied spontaneously to certain situations as a creative solution or resolution.

Maybe you can remember as a child having a "pretend friend" who accompanied you through lonely times and helped you transform them into enjoyable times. Children are able to look at a situation or an object and make believe it has more attributes than an adult sees. For example, when a new refrigerator is delivered, the adults usually throw out the cardboard container in which it was shipped and focus their attention on the new appliance. Children usually view the cardboard box as more interesting and enjoyable than the new refrigerator. It may become a playhouse in which they entertain their dolls and other toys, or a cabin, fort or castle in which they invite their friends to share the fantasy.

Take a peaceful moment to remember how much fun there can be in gazing through the looking glass of fantasy: to see the magic in the clouds, to wish on that "star light, star bright," to make believe that the large gray rock in the distance is a beautiful castle, to wear a paper ring and pretend it has lucky powers or can decode secret messages. Remember the magic you felt inside when hearing Jiminey Cricket sing, "When You Wish Upon a Star" in the classic animated version of *Pinocchio.*

After all, what is the real purpose of pretending except to change an unpleasant situation to one that is more tolerable and positive? By using the ability to pretend, you can teach your children to create their own solutions to their own problems. For example, when children who are experiencing a helpless feeling in their lives watch a cartoon such as Spider-Man, their own internal strengths may be activated to help them deal with their problems.

Referring back to our initial story of Davey and the Monster, Scooby Doo offers an excellent example of how children can use their natural ability to pretend. Since Scooby Doo is portrayed as a problem-solver, children can "pretend" to get the answer they need from him. Of course, what they are really doing is tapping into their own abilities to get answers instead of being "given" an answer by a parent, teacher or

**Figure 8**
Scooby Doo, as drawn by 8-year-old Billy

**Figure 9**
Scooby Doo, as drawn by 7-year-old Becky

therapist. By channeling their imaginations into the Scooby Doo character, children are free to discover answers for themselves, while still feeling the support and guidance of their parents. (Figures 8 and 9)

Through pretending cartoon fantasies, children not only become a part of the story, but the cartoon characters can continue to be a positive reminder for them that they have numerous abilities with which to help themselves. Pretending can change a world that appears hopeless to a child into one that is filled with hope.

By offering your children the following Pretend Techniques, you can become partners in creating a solid foundation for healthy problem solving. When your children are feeling worried, fearful or upset, select one of the following approaches.

### Pretend Technique #1:
### Seeing, Hearing and Feeling the Cartoon Friend

Select
Positive
Feeling

**Step 1:** When your child is having a problem, simply ask him, "What would you like to feel instead of the upset and worry you're having now?" Your child might respond that he would like to feel confident instead of scared about giving a class report the next day, for example.

Select
Cartoon
Friend

**Step 2:** Now have your child select a cartoon character who could help him feel the way he wants to feel. For example, one boy who was being mistreated by a school bully said that having the Hulk with him would make him feel safe. The cartoon characters selected by children represent those parts of themselves that can solve the problem.

Cartoon
Friend
Helps
Child

**Step 3:** Have your child close his eyes and pretend that he can see himself with his favorite cartoon friend. If your child wants confidence for a particular situation, for example, have him imagine the cartoon helper *looking* confident; then imagine the cartoon helper *feeling* confident; then imagine the cartoon helper *sounding* confident. Allow your child enough time to thoroughly imagine each phase of the cartoon friend looking, feeling and sounding confident.

Resolution

**Step 4:** Have your child pretend seeing the cartoon helper looking, feeling and sounding the way your child would like to be in his problem area. Then have your child imitate the cartoon character's abilities, and trade places, so he can experience his old problem in a new more positive way. In the example of a child needing confidence in giving a class report, he experiences the cartoon helper looking, feeling and sounding confident giving the report. He then trades places with the cartoon friend and continues giving the report with the look, feel and sound of *his own confidence.* Ask your child to open his eyes when he experiences the problem "all better."

Be sure to allow plenty of time for your child to visualize this last, important part. You might say, "Take all the time in the world you need to imagine all the new ways you can to fix that problem...feel better...learn that new skill, etc." Some children will take only a brief period of time while others will keep their eyes closed while imagining for a long time. Just sit quietly and be patient. Children will open their eyes when they have completed the experience.

This type of approach allows children to create

their own choices and solutions from their own inner resources of past positive experiences. By providing a framework that is familiar, such as the cartoon friend, you help them use what they have learned in the past to shape a more constructive future.

The second Pretend Technique is similar to the first. Your child's eyes should be closed comfortably throughout the following steps.

### Pretend Technique #2:
### Three Solutions from the Cartoon Helper

Select
Cartoon
Helper

**Step 1:** Begin by having your child close her eyes and select a favorite cartoon helper who can help her with her problem or worry. You might have your child nod her head once the cartoon helper is "available."

Three
Solutions

**Step 2:** Next, ask your child to pretend that the cartoon helper shows or tells her three ways to solve her problem. It may be helpful to have your child remember cartoons in which her favorite character "saved the day." Suggest that she nod her head when she has "received" this help. Again, some children may do this readily, while others will take more time. Just sit back and relax. Let your child take all the time she needs; the results will be far more effective.

The "Best Solution"

**Step 3:** Have your child select the one solution out of the three given by the cartoon helper that can best help her. Instruct your child to nod her head once she has selected that "best solution."

Resolution

**Step 4:** Finally, have your child imagine seeing herself using that "best solution" in the old problem area. Give her plenty of time, and gently encourage her to imagine this ending phase of the visualization in as much detail as possible. Tell her to open her eyes once the problem is "all better."

The power of these Pretend Techniques is that as children continue to see the cartoon helper on TV, in comic books, or in the form of a toy, it becomes an automatic, unconscious reminder for them of being protected and feeling confident and secure. Furthermore, you, the parent, become identified as the holder of that special key that opens these treasures and abilities within your children.

Artwork in its many forms has been used for centuries to help children and adults express their emotional responses to the various situations they encounter in their everyday lives. Nursery school teachers are well aware of the importance of integrating artwork into their classroom activities to provide relaxation, body awareness, and as a means to help children make visual what they experience in their lives. Artwork is a way to help children both express and separate from painful or difficult feelings. Drawing allows children to actually see what they are feeling; it also allows their own inner abilities to be made visual. Simply provide your children with colorful markers or crayons and a pad of plain paper. Pretend Technique #3 can be used as a guideline for adding another color in the rainbow of healthy problem solving.

### Pretend Technique #3:
### Drawing the Cartoon Helper

Draw
Problem

**Step 1:** On one sheet of paper, ask you child to draw a picture of what his worry, fear or pain looks like.

| | |
|---|---|
| Draw<br>Cartoon<br>Helper | **Step 2:** On a second sheet of paper, ask your child to draw a picture of the cartoon helper he knows could help him with his problem. |
| Draw<br>Problem<br>"All Better" | **Step 3:** On a third sheet, ask your child to draw how the problem would look when it is "all better." |

It can be helpful to ask children to look back at their first drawing and decide what they want to do with it. Some may want to keep it, while others may choose to crumble it or tear it and throw it away. The All Better pictures are children's own unconscious healing medicine reminding them that All Better does exist somewhere within them. You may want to create an album of these All Better pictures or hang them where your children can see them.

The following Pretend Technique can help interrupt a fearful experience of nightmares and monsters and turn it into one of mastery and success. It is similar to Pretend Technique #3, with the addition of presenting a gift to the fear.

### Pretend Technique #4
### The Cartoon Helper Selects a Gift.

| | |
|---|---|
| Draw<br>Problem | **Step 1:** Have your child draw what her fear looks like—its color, shape and size. |

41

| | |
|---|---|
| Draw Cartoon Helper | **Step 2:** Ask your child to select and draw a cartoon character that she knows can confront the fear and protect her. |
| Select Gift | **Step 3:** Now have your child and the cartoon helper together select and draw a gift to present to the fear which will "turn it into what you want it to be." The child might ask the cartoon character, "What would be the most powerful gift to give that monster so that we can become friends?" |
| Resolution | **Step 4:** After the gift is selected and presented to the fear, ask your child to draw how the fear has changed into a friend. This makes the change more visual. |

When children are experiencing pain or discomfort, they are in a "negative feeling place." By asking them what the pain looks like or sounds like, they can begin to separate from it, to feel more control over it, and to feel more comfortable about it.

The following Pretend Technique can be used in your own way to help your children change a painful experience into one that is more comfortable. Children can choose to do this exercise with their eyes either opened or closed.

## Pretend Technique #5
## Imagine the Cartoon Helper

| | |
|---|---|
| Visualize the Pain | **Step 1:** Ask your child to imagine what the pain looks like, that is, its color, shape or size: "If your pain could be seen, what would it look like?" |
| Hear the Pain | **Step 2:** Now have your child imagine what the pain sounds like, that is, its noise, tone or quality: "If your pain could make a noise, what would it sound like?" |
| Select Cartoon Helper | **Step 3:** Next, ask your child to select his favorite cartoon friend who has the ability to help him with his pain. |
| Imagine Problem "All Better" | **Step 4:** Finally, ask your child to imagine his favorite cartoon friend helping him change the look and sound of the pain into something more pleasant to see and hear: "How does |

that pain now look and sound "all better"?

Some children particularly enjoy making up stories ("My dog ate my homework"). They like listening to their own voices. Their imaginations seem to come to life, filling the room with the sound of images. With the next Pretend Technique, children have an opportunity to retell their problem in a new way—a way that includes a helpful cartoon friend and a positive ending. The retelling of the story can be directly told to you, handwritten or typed into a computer by the child, or told into a tape recorder.

### Pretend Technique #6:
### Storytelling

| | |
|---|---|
| Select Cartoon Helper | **Step 1:** Ask your child to select and describe a cartoon character who she knows is powerful enough to help her with her problems. She may select any type of character, ranging from lovable Mickey Mouse to the powerful Superheroes. |
| Select Resources | **Step 2:** Have your child describe what actions she sees the cartoon helper |

taking to change her problems. You can remind your child of all the problems, suspenses or "cliff hangers" shown in her favorite cartoon shows. The cartoon characters with the problem at first feel there is no solution, but finally that special hero arrives to "save the day." Examples of possible resources are Papa Smurf's magical potions, Dungeon Master's magical powers, etc.

There is an additional option for those using tape recorders. After your children have thoroughly described their new ending with the help of their cartoon friend, play back the recording for them to hear. They can listen with their eyes either open or closed—whichever is more comfortable. They may want to play the recording before falling asleep for a few nights.

Children may choose different cartoon heroes for different types of problems. The value in this is that each cartoon hero actually represents a different aspect of the children's own inner strengths and abilities. The children begin to act as if they were the heroes, and in the process, they learn how to draw upon their own resources. Eventually the cartoon helpers will simply fade away as the children internalize the qualities they see in the characters.

There is no end to the Pretend Techniques that you yourself can create by letting your own imagination add new shades of color to the rainbow of abilities within your children.

# 5

# FEELING DIFFERENT

# "It's Not Easy Being Green."

Looking back to our own childhoods, we can all remember how important it was to feel a part of a group. No matter what age, it was always important to have the same toys, clothes, bicycles and records as our friends. It was important to have that special feeling of belonging and acceptance. In any age group, there are always those who are leaders and those who are followers. The important point is not that leading is better than following, or vice versa, but that both leaders and followers learn to respect and appreciate their own special abilities. Some children deal with their individuality more easily than others. We can all agree that the ability not to follow the crowd, to sometimes say no, is a major learning we want to impart to our children for their healthy growth into adolescence and adulthood.

Parents often struggle with how they can help when their children feel left out or different from their friends. Children worried about their size, shape, color or background feel just as different as the physically handicapped child or the learning-disabled child.

49

Whatever the cause of felling different, children need to learn positive ways to deal with it.

When Jim Hensen introduced Kermit the Frog singing "It's Not Easy Being Green," children's social consciousness began to expand in ways that are still being appreciated today. The many lovable and funny Muppet characters that have followed Kermit offer a bright array of emotion, humor, and education that touch the lives and embrace the hearts of millions of children and parents throughout the world.

The issue of Feeling Different was also addressed in an episode of The Flintstones cartoon series. In this episode a "monster" family moves next door to Fred and Wilma. Fred is angry because those "weirdos" are on his block, and he does not want to make friends with them. However, Wilma insists on going next door with Fred and Pebbles for a welcome visit and bringing a gift. Many conflicts arise during the episode, especially when Fred's friends, Barney and Betty, go on a picnic with the new neighbors, overlooking their differences in favor of friendship. Fred also goes on the picnic, but refuses to be part of the group, thereby isolating himself and his family from the fun. During the picnic, Pebbles becomes involved in a dangerous situation and needs to be rescued. At this crisis, the "monster" neighbor's abilities (his height and strength) are used to help save Pebbles. Fred is then able to see his neighbor in a different and more positive way, which opens the door for friendship to develop.

We view this cartoon as an excellent symbolic example of the process of confronting fears, dealing with anger and developing openness to people who are "different." Children can readily identify with both parts of the story line—being afraid of someone who is different and themselves being shunned as different. This particular cartoon episode is an example of how the not-so-perfect world we live in can be used as a means of teaching valuable skills in tolerance and interpersonal relating.

Another example of this type of "social metaphor" cartoon is the Fat Albert series created and produced by Bill Cosby, which portrays his childhood experiences in a humorous way. Cosby's characters are rich with their own personalities, presenting a much needed view of urban "street kid" life and the fun that children can experience through their own inventiveness and creativity. Here the cartoon serves children from the street, as well as those from more "sheltered" environments. The more sheltered children learn a new type of resourcefulness from the street kids' antics, and the street kids experience a sense of positive recognition, acceptance, and even pride. On a larger, social level, we could even go so far as to say that this series is contributing to a fundamental shift in identity and image for an important segment of our society by focusing on the positive aspects of "street life." Recognition in a humorous, positive way can match children's real-life experiences and convey the subliminal message of "You're OK."

An example of feeling different was that of a nine-year-old boy, Tommy, who was having serious behavior and peer problems in school. When Tommy spoke, his voice was low and sad. He explained, "The kids all pick on me and I don't do anything. They call me names and don't like me." Tommy was asked about his favorite cartoon shows. He said that he like Dungeons and Dragons, a cartoon show that was created from the popular game. He was then asked to describe what he liked best about the characters. Tommy spoke about an episode in which Eric was turned into a big monster, which was a very ugly creature that lived in the foreign land where Eric and his companions were lost. Although his friends wanted to return home, they gave up their chance to escape and stayed to help Eric through his crisis. Tommy saw these characters as being different, as each having special abilities, and as each being helpful to one another when there was trouble.

Following the guidelines of Pretend Technique #2: Three Solutions from the Cartoon Helper, Tommy was asked to close his eyes and nod when he was able to see his favorite Dungeons and Dragons characters.

He was then asked to have those characters whisper into his ear three ways to help him get along better with the children at school. He was instructed to take his time and to nod his head once he had received the three choices. After a few minutes, Tommy nodded his head, opened his eyes wide, and with a smile said, "Yeah, I got 'em!"

Tommy was told to close his eyes again and "pick the best of those three solutions that you know can help you get along better with your classmates. Nod your head when you are ready." Tommy paused for half a minute or so. After he nodded his head, he was asked to imagine seeing himself at school using the new solution from his cartoon friends: "Use that solution, Tommy, that you know can help you with those problems you've been having at school. And your eyes will open only after you have experienced that solution in a way that is comfortable for you."

When Tommy opened his eyes, there was a noticeable change in his expression from one of sadness to one of delight. Even the tonal quality of his voice was stronger, and he spoke with enthusiasm. There was no need to analyze or have Tommy verbalize exactly what he had been thinking. This was a purely internal experience in which Tommy could enter his own world and discover the abilities he needed to help him deal better with his problem. Some children may choose to tell their parents what they have experienced. Parents can simply let the children share their experiences while listening in a nonjudgmental and nonintrusive way.

Enjoy using the steps in this technique as a framework for engaging your own creative abilities in helping your children through the many struggles of feeling different. Allow them to become aware that "different" is just that; it is not good or bad, but simply different. In this way, you help them to feel loved and appreciated for their unique qualities.

# 6

# MONSTERS, MEANIES, AND NIGHTMARES

Maybe you remember as a child being afraid of the dark and needing a night-light. Sometimes there were fearful monsters in your bedroom or under your bed. Other times there were frightening nightmares that woke you up crying for help. It is important to help children deal with fearful experiences in a healthy way. Children will be exposed to many fearful situations and need to learn that fear is a part of life and can be overcome and mastered.

The essence of Yoda's teaching in *Return of the Jedi* was to confront the fear within (the dark side) rather than run from it. Just as Yoda counseled Luke to confront this dark side because the "force," too, would always be within, so have we found it helpful for children to do likewise. The "force" is each child's inheritance of resources, abilities and potentials which can be used to overcome whatever is threatening. Cartoon characters can show these two opposing parts of the child—the strengths and the fears—in symbolic ways. When effectively utilized, a cartoon sequence can actually be the "battleground of victory" in which children play out in their imagination a confrontation between themselves and their fear.

Cartoon villains and monsters have been a common target of criticism by many parent and education groups who are concerned with positive programming for children. However, children's imaginations create fiercer monsters and more gruesome scenes than most animators would ever dare to portray in cartoons. Furthermore, through these self-created monsters, children express the angry or fearful experiences of their own lives. Simply banning monster characters from cartoons is no solution, unless it coincides with a parallel banishment of monsters (difficulties, conflicts, challenges) in the everyday world. It is more to the point to find positive and creative ways to *utilize the monsters in a manner that promotes growth and mastery.*

One easy utilization of cartoon monsters occurs through what could be called the "dilution effect." A cartoon monster can dilute the potency of a child's self-created monster simply because animators and writers control the outcome of the story. In a child's imagination, a monster can do *anything,* but in a cartoon script, the monster only does *certain things,* which are then foiled by the cartoon hero.

Fear in the form of monsters is one of the most common problems for children. One effective method for dealing with such monsters is to have children confront them in their imaginations and present a gift as a token of friendship. Making friends with the monsters means making friends with (overcoming) the fear.

We used this technique with Daniele, a seven-year-old girl who had sleeping problems. She said she was unable to sleep well because there were monsters in her bedroom. At this point we told her the "true, untold story" of monsters.

### The Monster and the Cupcake

Matching
: Daniele was told that the monsters were really children who had no one to play with and had no friends. They felt sad and did not know how to get attention from anyone. So one day they decided that if they dressed in a bizarre way and acted strangely, people would pay attention. When they appeared dressed in weird clothes and acting in weird ways, people became frightened and called them "monsters."

Resources
: Daniele was reminded of the story of ET and how Elliot presented him a

gift of Reeses Pieces to make friends. She was then told to "go home and give your monsters a gift."

Solutions

When she returned the next week, her mother reported that Daniele had made a cupcake, presented it to the monster at bedtime, and slept through the night for the first time in years.

The gift in this technique represents children's own inner resources, which are now activated in the positive process of confronting the monster (the fear). In giving a gift to the monster, a negative experience of fear is thus transformed into a positive experience of courage and victory. Moreover, since children must dip into their own bank of creativity to select and make the gift, many untapped resources are automatically stimulated which can then be transformed to other areas of their lives. After successfully befriending their own monster, children may then be better able to relate to school friends, or they may feel more confident generally to attempt many new things. We frequently receive reports from parents about delightful "bonus" effects of this technique. It seems that the positive effects spread into other areas in which children were previously "stuck."

**Figure 10**
E.T., as drawn by 7-year-old Becky

What is the role of the cartoon character in such an approach? The cartoon character can be used as a kind of ready-made support system, one coming entirely from the child's own inner world. Children can carry out the activity of selecting, creating and presenting their gift to the monster with the cartoon hero at their side. Or, they can have the cartoon hero function as their proxy in presenting the gift. In either case, the cartoon hero is a safe "third medium," which provides support, guidance and companionship. These qualities become available to children in their everyday lives once they have been stimulated to the surface through the agency of the cartoon hero.

When you acknowledge and respect your children's perception of situations, they learn to feel a sense of "OK-ness." To tell children who are experiencing nightmares, "You shouldn't be afraid, there are no such things as monsters," may create confusion, more fear and mistrust. However, parents can align and match themselves with their children's reality by attempting to see what it is the children see. In this way, parents help their children discover ways of feeling safe and secure. Many times, just letting children discuss the frightening nightmare helps to relieve tension.

By asking them to select a favorite cartoon character (using one of the six Pretend Techniques) who can successfully protect them, you introduce a powerful ally into the situation. Children have seen that cartoon character on TV repeatedly "save the day" and thwart the monster.

An example of using Pretend Technique #4: The Cartoon Helper Selects A Gift, was seen in Timmy, a 10-year-old boy who had been experiencing terrifying nightmares for several years. His parents would let him sleep in their room because of his screaming and fear associated with the nightmares. He was given a box of crayons and asked to draw what that fear looked like. (Figure 11)

Timmy was then instructed to select and draw the cartoon character he knew would confront the fear and protect him. He immediately described Mr. T as his protector. (Figure 12)

Next, Timmy and his cartoon friend, Mr. T, were asked to draw a gift they could present to the fear which would turn it into what he wanted it to be. "Timmy, what would be the most powerful gift you and Mr. T could give to that scary feeling (the monster) so that you could become friends?" He took the crayon and drew a picture representing money. At first it was $20, then he made it into $1 million. (Figure 13)

Finally, Timmy drew how his fear now looked after receiving the $1,000,000 from him and Mr. T. (Figure 14)

**Figure 11**
Timmy's School Fear

**Figure 12**
Timmy's Cartoon Helper, Mr. T

**Figure 13**
Timmy's Gift to the Monster

66

**Figure 14**
Timmy's Fear "All Better"

Timmy, himself, was given a gift of a one dollar bill in Monopoly money and the suggestion to use a crayon to change it into a $1,000,000 dollar bill. It was further suggested that Timmy take the $1,000,000 dollar bill to school and look at it whenever he needed to be reminded of how Mr. T could help him.

Timmy's selection of Mr. T brings up the controversial subject of the affect of cartoon viewing on children. Do aggressive cartoon heroes have an adverse affect on children's behavior? In our experience, Mr. T, The Incredible Hulk, Spider-Man, and all their counterparts can have a positive value for children when used wisely. We have never known the positive use of a powerful cartoon character to cause a behavior or acting-out problem. In Timmy's case, he needed someone big and strong to match and confront the terror he felt about school; Mr. T served that purpose. Timmy did not imitate Mr. T in any behavior. Rather, Mr. T seemed to activate Timmy's own self-confidence by functioning as a secret friend rather than as a behavior model.

Another example of how cartoon characters can help children with fear can be seen in how 7-year-old Matthew used Pretend Technique #3, Drawing the Cartoon Helper, to help him with his fear of the dark. (Figures 15, 16 and 17)

**Figure 15**
Matthew's Fear of the Dark

**Figure 16**
Matthew's Cartoon Helper, Woody Woodpecker

**Figure 17**
Matthew's Fear "All Better"

# 7

# "MOMMY, KISS IT AND MAKE IT BETTER"

Children often come home with skinned knees or other hurts and ask Mommy or Daddy for a kiss to "make it better." The magic of these kisses helps comfort children through numerous childhood illnesses such as mumps, chicken pox, colds, sore throats, toothaches, earaches, tummy aches, and sometimes even hospitalization for various injuries or more serious illnesses. The "magic" in those kisses of the parents is the loving concern and the help all parents want to offer their children when they are hurting in some way.

Here again the cartoon friend can be of great help to children, parents, teachers and even physicians. For example, when children need to go to the doctor for medical treatment, they may be frightened and put up a fuss about going for help. Parents can simply ask, "What cartoon friend would you like to have with you now who can help you feel better?" If the child replies, "Mickey Mouse," for example, the parent can say, "Good, let's take a minute and imagine taking Mickey with us to the doctor's office. Maybe the doctor can help Mickey, too." If the children have an actual toy of the cartoon character, they can be encouraged to take it along with them while receiving treatment. The cartoon friend can thus become the children's comforter similar to those magical kisses of the parents.

An example of how you can use cartoon characters as your "kisses" during those times when your children may be ill is illustrated by Suzie, a delightful eight-year-old girl who was hospitalized for tests because she was experiencing pain in the area of her kidneys. Thus far the tests were not revealing any physical cause for the pain. Her mother, Rita, was present in the room at the time when little Suzie explained in a low, shaky voice, "It hurts here," pointing to her kidneys. She was asked to imagine seeing what the pain looked like and to describe what she saw (Pretend Technique #5). Suzie replied, "It's a circle and it's red." Suzie was then asked who was her favorite cartoon character who she knew could help make the pain all better. Her face brightened as Suzie replied with an enthusiastic voice, "Wonder Woman. She makes me feel strong." The expression on Suzie's face and the tone in her voice became happily animated as she spoke more about Wonder Woman.

A story was then made up about how nice it would be to be with Wonder Woman right now. It was suggested that Suzie take a few deep comfortable breaths in through her nose and out through her mouth to help her to relax. She was then asked to look out the window and imagine seeing herself and Wonder Woman playing, laughing and having fun. Suzie followed the suggestions and her expression transformed into one of happiness.

Later that day Suzie became worried about being all alone in the hospital overnight. Remembering the previous story, her mother made up her own story using Wonder Woman as the main character. After a while, Rita noticed the expression on Suzie's face change from one of tension and fear to one of happiness and relaxation.

The next day, Suzie's mother commented that using these techniques made it easier for her to leave the hospital that night because she found a way to help Suzie feel more comfortable. This is important because parents often feel helpless when their children are hurting. These approaches can replace those feelings of helplessness with feelings of hopefulness.

Since many children enjoy drawing, you might prefer to follow the framework of Pretend Technique #3, Drawing the Cartoon Helper. The following illustrations were drawn by Suzie as part of a book she created during her hospital stay. Suzie entitled her creative idea, "My Pain Getting Better Book."

| | |
|---|---|
| Draw The Pain | **Step 1:** Suzie was asked to draw a picture of what the pain looks and/or sounds like. (Figure 18) |
| Draw Cartoon Helper | **Step 2:** Suzie was then asked to draw a picture of her favorite cartoon friend who she knew could help make the pain feel better. Suzie selected Wonder Woman. (Figure 19) |
| Draw Problem "All Better" | **Step 3:** Suzie was then asked to draw a picture of how the pain would look and/or sound "all better." (Figure 20) |

Imaginary cartoon friends can help activate children's strengths and decrease the level of their fear and pain. With these added skills, you and your children become partners in the healing process.

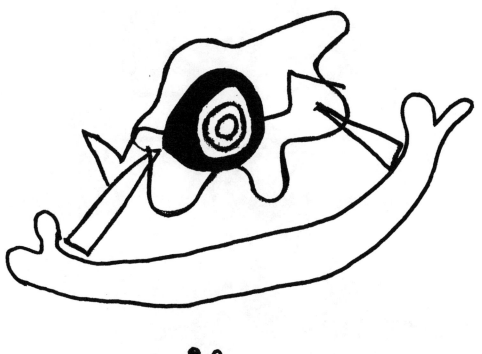

**Figure 18**
Suzie's Pain

**Figure 19**
Suzie's Cartoon Helper, Wonder Woman

PAIN All BeTTer

**Figure 20**
Suzie's Pain "All Better"

# 8

# TRANSITION, CHANGE, AND LOSS

Children encounter times of transition, change and loss as naturally as the seasons change from spring to summer, from fall to winter. However, they may not always feel the comfort they would like to feel, or the security they need to feel, when making that change. For example, many times teachers are aware of behavioral changes in their children at the beginning and end of school years. Children are aware of moving on to the next grade and may not be feeling secure about this expected transition. Some may experience moodiness, or may return to acting out younger behaviors they had long outgrown, such as bedwetting or baby talk. Certainly parents notice the change in their older children when a newborn sister or brother is brought into the home.

This situation can be seen in the dilemma of a seven-year-old boy, Peter. (Peter's problem was helped by blending Pretend Technique #3: Drawing, and Pretend Technique #6: Storytelling.) He had developed a number of fears and concerns following the birth of a brother and the subsequent changes in his family life.

Peter had become more and more attached to his mother and demanded more and more of her attention. Whenever his mother needed to leave the home and he was left with a babysitter, Peter would become extremely fearful and tearful. Seeing her son in such emotional pain created guilt in his mother. Even at school, Peter found it difficult to make the transition from mother to teacher. He was described by the teacher as daydreaming much of the time.

Peter was presented crayons and drawing paper and asked to "draw that worry you have when Mommy is not with you." As he was drawing, he began to talk about the drawing. Peter was automatically entering his own inner world of imagination as he was making up a story. He was encouraged to continue creating his story. (Figure 21)

He was then asked to introduce a cartoon character into his story who could change his conflict of aloneness and fear into a happy ending of safeness and security. As he talked, he began drawing Ice Man and the Hulk. Selecting the cartoon characters and drawing them implied for Peter, on an unconscious level, that security and safety were available to him in some way when he was not with his mother. (Figure 22)

Peter continued rambling about how Ice Man and the Hulk were powerful. He described in detail

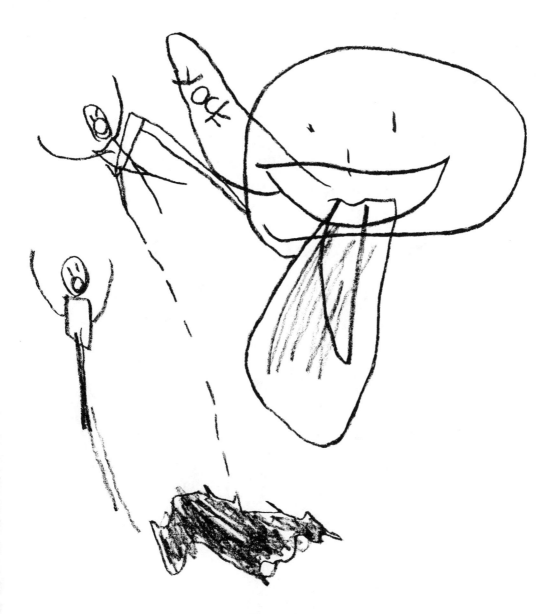

**Figure 21**
Peter's Worry

87

**Figure 22**
Peter's Cartoon Helpers, Ice Man and the Hulk

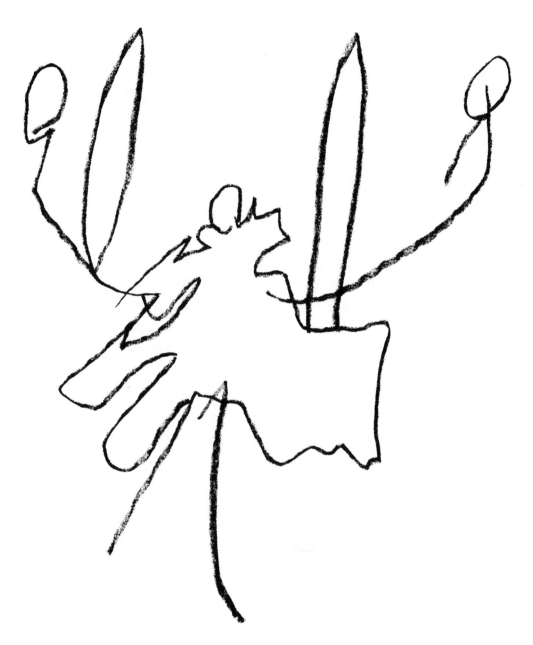

**Figure 23**
Peter's Worry "All Better"

how they overcame the "bad guys" (the bad feelings) all the time. Once again he was encouraged to give all the examples he wanted of the abilities and strengths of Ice Man and the Hulk.

On a third piece of paper, Peter drew how his "worry looks all better" now that Ice Man and the Hulk have helped. He eagerly drew and continued telling his story containing solutions and resolutions. (Figure 23)

Possibly for the first time in months, Peter was no longer stuck in his painful experience of fear. He had created his own resources (Ice Man and the Hulk) and solutions (security and safety). Now, whenever he daydreams about his separation from his mother, he has available positive thoughts (his verbal story) and positive pictures (the resource and solution drawings) to support him. These new therapeutic ingredients can help to interrupt his previous painful feeling of separation, change and transition, and start to blend into feelings of safety and security.

What happens when the separation or loss is caused by a special friend or teacher moving away? Possibly an older brother leaves home for college or moves to another town. Perhaps a favorite relative dies. Sometimes the parents become divorced, or a parent may even die. Issues of death, dying and separation are not easy subjects for parents to present to

90

their children. However, if provided with helpful techniques, parents can become more comfortable and open in helping their children face such experiences. Here again, the cartoon helper can become a comfort to grieving children in the same way that the special blanket, teddy bear or stuffed animal is carried around for support.

The experience of loss was well illustrated in a cartoon episode of the Smurfs, in which Smurfette's pet mouse died. In the sequences that followed, each of the characters in the cartoon expressed an important stage of the loss process. In the beginning, there was disbelief—Smurfette refused to believe that her mouse had died—followed by anger, sadness, guilt, and finally resolution. The episode ended with Smurfette learning to accept loss as a natural part of life. The beauty of this episode was that it portrayed in a positive way the full range of emotions connected with the difficult experience of death. Because the cartoon story and characters are not "real," they enable children to view experiences such as death in a detached manner. The story provides a safe vehicle for children to experience the loss, while learning on another level valuable ways to cope with it.

Certainly the fear of losing a friend, loved one or pet creates great worry within a child. Parents may notice behavioral and emotional changes such as sleeping problems, moodiness, angry outbursts, withdrawl or excessive clingingness.

Those of us who saw the movie ET may remember our feelings of fear while sitting at the edge of our seats when Elliot and ET were battling with staying alive. That feeling of fear of losing someone or something we love needs special attention and help.

The drawings below were done by our friend Suzie, about a year after her hospital visit. Her dog, Pockets, was dying and she was struggling with her fears and sadness about this important loss. Following the steps in Pretend Technique #3, Drawing the Cartoon Helper, Suzie was asked to draw how her fear and sadness looked. (Figure 24)

She was then asked to draw what cartoon character would help her feel better while she was dealing with this problem. Suzie chose Fred Flintstone, and drew him. (Figure 25)

She was then asked to draw the "fear" looking "all better." (Figure 26)

Afterward Suzie stated, "I was drawing pictures of what it felt like when my dog died. Then I drew Fred Flintstone. Then me and Fred together so I would feel better after my dog died."

Another example of dealing with loss using cartoons and their characters occurred with a delightful

**Figure 24**
Suzie's Fear and Sadness

**Figure 25**
Suzie's Cartoon Helper, Fred Flintstone

94

**Figure 26**
Suzie's Fear "All Better"

eight-year-old girl named Erica. Erica's mother had died and her father was unable to care for her; therefore, she lived with foster parents. Her foster mother reported that Erica seemed to cry for no reason and showed frequent mood shifts from happiness to sadness. She also wanted to be with her foster mother most of the time.

We felt that Erica's behavior was directly related to her painful losses. After establishing a good rapport with her, we asked her about her favorite cartoon character—one that made her feel happy when she saw it. She readily talked about Smurfette and the other Smurf characters. A story was then constructed which used these cartoon characters to depict similar losses, thereby matching Erica's problem, and to depict ways of dealing with loss in a healthy way, thereby stimulating her own inner resources and strengths to do the same.

After a few sessions using this approach, Erica was asked to draw a picture. She drew a picture of a rainbow with Smurf holding a ball with a happy face in the center and a few raindrops in the upper corner. When asked about the raindrops she said, "There are only a few raindrops now because the rainbow is coming out." This indicated to us that the story utilizing the Smurf character had successfully evoked her strengths (the rainbow), and had established a positive association or model which would eventually clear up all the raindrops (tears) as the rainbow came out fully. (Figure 27)

**Figure 27**
Erica's Cartoon Helper, a Smurf, with the Rainbow

98

# 9

# CARTOON
# RATING
# SCALE

While we believe strongly in the positive potential of cartoons for children in general, we also recognize the need for an evaluation of cartoons for each child as an individual. What may be frightening and uncomfortable for one child may be therapeutic and transforming for another. It may be better for one child not to watch a particular cartoon sequence, while for another child, it may be a way of working out fear and anxieties. We believe that discriminations of this nature can be made only while the child is actually watching the cartoon. We have developed a Cartoon Rating Scale to assist parents in learning to recognize the cartoons and their characters that are helpful for their particular children. By using this scale, parents can learn how to observe and evaluate their children's reactions.

It is our experience that children know what they like, what makes them feel good, and what may frighten them. Parents can learn to recognize their children's reactions to the cartoons and how to use that information to help their children in many areas of their lives. The Cartoon Rating Scale can be applied to TV shows, movies and other situations that arise in children's lives.

This scale, which is designed specifically for parents to use with their individual children, is far more effective for use in one's personal life than a scale or monitoring system designed by a children's interest group. Group findings are based on normative reactions. This means substituting numbers for human realities, and substituting group averages for individual needs and preferences.

Often parents are concerned with the fighting, punching, yelling or hitting that is portrayed in cartoons. For some children, cartoons depicting physical bouts may be a release, a way of dealing with a situation symbolically which matches their own emotions within their life. The key word in the previous sentence is "symbolically." In other words, the hitting or yelling being shown can symbolically represent an expression of anger, but does not necessarily mean to children that all angry situations are handled by hitting or punching.

For example, children having behavior problems, that is children who "act out" their anger and fear, could be encouraged to make up a story about The Incredible Hulk. They would be reminded that the Hulk only comes out when he or someone else is in danger. Even the Hulk knows the difference between pointless destruction and self-protection. With this as a foundation, alternative ways of dealing with anger and fear can be introduced, again using the Hulk's continual search for his own "cure" as a parallel to the children's search for their own "cure" in their real life situations.

What is helpful for one child may be overwhelming for another. By using an individualized Cartoon Rating Scale, parents can participate actively and accurately as guides and helpers in their children's world of cartoon fantasy.

## CARTOON RATING SCALE

| | |
|---|---|
| Selection | Select cartoon show and view it with your children. |
| Observation | Simply observe your children's mood and behavior during the cartoon show. Note your children's overall emotional reactions to that episode. Are they happy, scared, relaxed, fidgety, etc.? |
| Discussion | Then have your children discuss which cartoon character was their favorite one and, specifically, what |

they liked about the character. Some children may select more than one favorite cartoon character. Younger children may enjoy watching the cartoon with their favorite toy, doll or teddy bear, and may wish to communicate their experience through their toy: "My dolly likes it."

Drawing

Next, present your children with drawing implements such as crayons or markers and ask them to draw their general reaction to the cartoon show. If the children experienced happiness or fear, for example, ask them to "draw how that feeling looks—how it looks to you."

Applications

Save your children's drawing. They can show the range of their emotional reactions to the cartoon, such as happy *and* scared. When reviewing future cartoons, comic books, TV shows, movies, etc., you can present drawings to your children and they can select the ones that best describe their present reactions. In this way, children become their own monitors with your help.

Your can further utilize the Cartoon Rating Scale's list of positive cartoon characters and experiences that evoke happy, safe and secure feelings within your children. You can use this list of positive associations in the Pretend Techniques as well as in creating your own stories to help your children interrupt their experiences of fears, discomfort, pain, nightmares, sleeplessness. etc.

By using the Cartoon Rating Scale, you will know what cartoon shows your children can safely watch and can circle them in the television viewing guides for your children to follow.

We strongly believe that the art of drawing and animation known as the cartoon can enter a new era of social and therapeutic usefulness. Cartoonists and animators, together with concerned parents, educators, therapists, nurses and physicians, can become part of the "growing edge" of changing human consciousness. The possibilities for the creation and the utilization of truly therapeutic cartoons are limited only by the number of children in the world.

105

# CARTOON RATING SCALE

| CHILD'S NAME | CARTOON SHOW | CHILD'S REACTIONS | FAVORITE CARTOON CHARACTER(S) | MOST LIKED ABOUT FAVORITE CHARACTER(S) |
|---|---|---|---|---|
| | | | | |

DRAWING OF CHILD'S OVERALL REACTION

# CARTOON RATING SCALE

| CHILD'S NAME | CARTOON SHOW | CHILD'S REACTIONS | FAVORITE CARTOON CHARACTER(S) | MOST LIKED ABOUT FAVORITE CHARACTER(S) |
|---|---|---|---|---|
| | | | | |

DRAWING OF CHILD'S OVERALL REACTION

# CARTOON RATING SCALE

| CHILD'S NAME | CARTOON SHOW | CHILD'S REACTIONS | FAVORITE CARTOON CHARACTER(S) | MOST LIKED ABOUT FAVORITE CHARACTER(S) |
|---|---|---|---|---|
|  |  |  |  |  |

DRAWING OF CHILD'S OVERALL REACTION

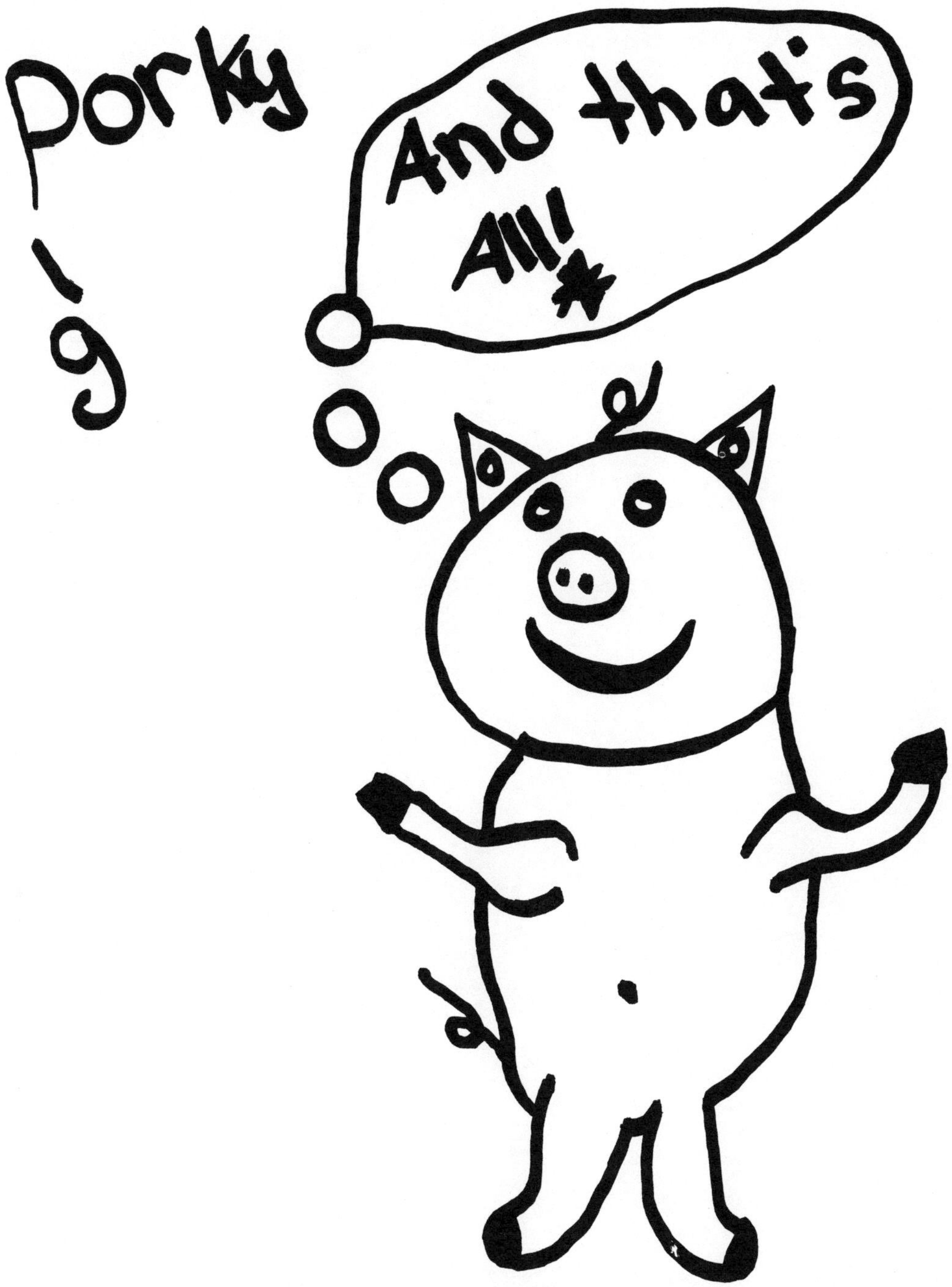
Porky
9
And that's All!